NATIVE ✳ AMERICAN ✳ CULTURE

SPIRITUAL LIFE

Victoria Sherrow

Series Editor
Jordan E. Kerber, Ph.D.

✳ ✳ ✳

ROURKE PUBLICATIONS, INC.
Vero Beach, Florida 32964

©1994 by Rourke Publications, Inc.

Printed in the United States of America.

A Blackbirch Graphics book.

Library of Congress Cataloging-in-Publication Data

Sherrow, Victoria
Spiritual Life / by Victoria Sherrow.
    p. cm. — (Native American culture)
    Includes bibliographical references and index.
    ISBN 0-86625-538-9
    1. Indians of North America—Religion 2. Indians of North America—Rites and ceremonies. I. Title. II. Series.
E98.R3S43   1994
299'.7—dc20
                                    94-5529
                                      CIP
                                      AC

Contents

Introduction

The words "Native Americans" and "Indians" create strong images for many people. Some may think of fierce warriors with bows and arrows, tomahawks, and rifles who battled the U.S. Cavalry in the days of the Wild West. Others probably imagine a proud and peaceful people who just hunted buffalo and lived in tipis on the Great Plains. These are just some of the popular stereotypes of Native Americans, and like most stereotypes they give a false impression.

This series on *Native American Culture* presents six books on various aspects of Native American life: child rearing, arts and crafts, daily life, tribal law, spiritual life, and the invasion by Europe. By reading these books, you will learn that there is no single Native American culture, but instead many different ones. Each Native American group or tribe in the past, as well as today, is a separate nation. While tribes may share some similarities, many are as different from one another as the English are from the Spanish.

The geographic focus of this series is the North American continent (United States and Canada), with special attention to the area within the present-day United States. However, Native Americans have lived, and continue to live, in Central America and South America. In addition, the authors of each book draw upon a wealth of historical information mainly from a time between the 1500s and 1900s, when most Native Americans were first contacted by European explorers, conquerors, and settlers. Much is known about this period of Native American life from documents and observations recorded by Europeans who came to North America.

It is also important to understand that Native Americans have a much longer and more complex history on the continent than just the past 500 years. Archaeologists have excavated ancient Native American sites as old as 12,000 years. The people who lived at these sites were among the first residents of North America. They did not keep written records of their lives, so the only information known about them comes from their stone tools and other remains that they left behind. We do know that during the thousands of years of Native American settlement across the continent the cultures of these early inhabitants changed in many important ways. Some of these cultures disappeared a long time ago, while others have survived and continue to change today. Indeed, there are more than 1.5 million Native Americans currently living in the United States, and the federal government recognizes over 500 tribes. Native Americans are in all walks of life, and many still practice traditions and speak the languages of their ancestors. About 250,000 Native Americans presently live on some 278 reservations in the country.

The books in this series capture the wonderful richness and variety of Native American life from different time periods. They remind us that the story of America begins with Native Americans. They also provide more accurate images of Native Americans, images that I hope will enable you to challenge the stereotypes.

Jordan E. Kerber, Ph.D.
Director of Native American Studies
Colgate University

Chapter

1

Ancient Traditions

How did life begin, and what is its purpose? How was the Earth created? What happens when we die? For thousands of years, people all over the world have wondered about these questions. The beliefs that people hold about the creation of the world and the meaning of life are often described as spiritual matters, or religion.

Native American religions are among the oldest and most deeply rooted in the world. Beliefs in unseen forces and spirits greater than themselves shaped Native Americans' attitudes about the world and the ways they lived. In 1855, a young Cayuse chief summed up his basic beliefs by saying, "The Great Spirit, in placing men on the Earth, desired them to take good care of the ground and to do each other no harm."

The rich spirituality of Native American peoples has survived since ancient times. Archaeologists—scientists who study ways of life in the past—have dug up places where

Native Americans lived more than 10,000 years ago. Although archaeologists have difficulty studying ancient Native American religions because Native Americans did not have written languages in ancient times, objects and burial sites give clues about how ancient peoples practiced their religions. Through the centuries, legends and stories, sometimes called myths, have also been handed down orally to new generations by tribal elders. Native Americans prize their commitment to oral (spoken) history, a strong force in keeping their religious traditions alive.

An ancient Native American burial site reveals a collection of pottery as well as animal and human remains. Modern archaeologists learn a great deal about ancient customs and religious practices from studying burial site artifacts.

Beliefs and Practices

Although Native American religions differ among tribes, there are also many similarities that are shared, both with one another and with major religions around the world. Native American societies believed that a Supreme Being or Creator (sometimes called the Great Spirit) created the world and all the forces of nature. Creation stories told how the Earth and all living things came to be. Native Americans also believed in a variety of other spirits. They often looked beyond death to an afterlife, since they believed humans had an eternal spirit as well as a physical body. Similar to other religions, tribal members took part in acts of worship, offering prayers to spiritual beings whom they believed had power over the Earth.

Like other peoples, Native Americans tried to understand why the world held both good and evil, as well as sorrow and joy. Tribal legends gave various explanations for the human condition. To please the Creator or Great Spirit, people were supposed to follow rules that told them how to behave. Along with these morals, there were several taboos—forbidden behaviors. Tribes also told stories that gave reasons for their particular beliefs and practices. Many groups thought certain truths or sacred objects had been given to their tribe directly from the higher spirits themselves.

As with some other religions, Native American beliefs included prophecies—predictions about the future. Certain spiritually gifted people, called prophets, were thought to be able to tell what was ahead. It was said that prophets were sent by the Great Spirit. Some prophets strongly influenced their tribes. For example, the prophet Deganawidah led five warring tribes to agree to the Great Peace, uniting to form the Iroquois Confederacy, or Iroquois League.

While sharing traits with other religions—belief in a higher power, creation stories, a moral code, a creed (set of

beliefs), acts of worship, prophecies, and belief in an after-life—Native American religions are unique. Spirituality is much more closely tied to daily activities than is typical of most religions, particularly in modern times. Often, one cannot separate a tribe's religion from its culture, or way of life. This is especially true of some groups, such as the Hopi, where prayers take place throughout the day and even the designs of their homes and villages on the desert mesas reflect spiritual beliefs.

Much has been said about the way Native American cultures lived. They felt a connection to all things, living and dead, and sought to coexist with, rather than to control, the Earth. According to Native American tradition, all things have a purpose for being. A balance must be kept between living creatures and the places where they live. Since all of creation reveals the greatness of the Creator, nature connects humankind to the Great Spirit.

At One with Nature

Native Americans saw the world itself as a place of worship. A Santee Sioux named Ohiyesa, also known as Charles Alexander Eastman, made this romanticized speech in 1911:

> In the life of the Indian . . . daily devotions were more necessary to him than daily food. He wakes at daybreak, puts on his moccasins and steps down to the water's edge. Here he throws handfuls of clear, cold water into his face or plunges in bodily. After the bath, he stands erect before the advancing dawn, facing the sun as it dances upon the horizon. . . . Whenever in the course of the daily hunt the red hunter comes upon a scene that is strikingly beautiful or sublime—a black thundercloud with the rainbow's glowing arch above the mountain, a white waterfall in the heart of a green gorge, a vast prairie tinged with the blood-red of sunset—he pauses for an instant in the attitude of worship. He sees no need for setting apart one day in seven as a holy day, since to him all days are God's.

Opposite:
The beautiful ruins of Cliff Palace at Mesa Verde National Park were once home to the Anasazi, ancestors of the Pueblo peoples. The design of these homes reflected the Anasazi's deep connection to the Earth.

✳

12

Native Americans also viewed many things on Earth as being like a circle. The seasons of the year came and went; the sun rose and set each day, giving life on Earth unity and a rhythmic quality. Even a person's life followed this pattern, as he or she went from being a baby to an adult to being helpless like a baby again in old age. The cycles of life were viewed as timeless and connected, year after year, not a string of separate events. Having, or acquiring, new things was not necessarily an objective for Native Americans.

Because of their beliefs, many Native Americans earned praise for owning nothing or giving their horses or goods to others. Personal wealth might be measured in terms of acts of kindness, courage, or spiritual strength, not material goods. This attitude led to conflicts with the white settlers of North America, who saw humans as beings superior to animals, meant to own land, and adapt nature for human purposes.

Native Americans found great spiritual meaning through their relationships with their homelands. These ancestral lands, with their distinctive plants, animals, birds, and geographic features, were the subjects of tribal religious stories. Legends explained how a tribe had come to live on its lands. Legends also told of the purpose of the other creatures and things Native Americans found on their lands. Sacred sites, or places, on the lands were used for worship during the year. Burial sites were also honored. As Chief Seattle of the Suquamish-Duwamish tribe said in 1855, "To us the ashes of our ancestors are sacred and their resting place is hallowed ground."

Later, in 1900, Cecilio Blacktooth explained the great importance of tribal lands:

> You ask us to think what place we would like next best to this place, where we always lived. You see the graveyard out there? There are our fathers and our grandfathers. You see

that Eagle-next mountain and that Rabbit-hole mountain? When God made them, He gave us this place. We have always been here. We do not care for any other place. . . . We have always lived here. We would rather die here. Our fathers did. We cannot leave them. Our children were born here—How can we go away? If you give us the best place in the world, it is not so good for us as this.

Spirit Helpers

Another major trait of Native American religions was that people frequently called upon various spirits for help. Spirits were asked to keep the Earth fertile, so crops would grow and animals abound, supplying people with food. For the Pueblo peoples of the desert Southwest, rain and water spirits were vital. Ceremonies were often held to create and maintain proper relationships with these forces. Many ceremonies gave thanks for food and other necessities. Healing the sick was also done in a religious atmosphere.

Different kinds of spiritual leaders guided a tribe, including priests, shamans, and medicine men or healers, among others. Other villagers could become part of groups that participated in important ceremonies, such as the Snake Society of the Hopi that performed the Snake Dance, or the Buffalo Societies of the Plains Indians. Individuals could hope to become closer to the spirits through a dream or vision, or by attracting a guardian spirit who would be their special helper throughout life.

Clashing Cultures

By the 1500s, when white people landed on the shores of North America, there were hundreds of thousands of Native Americans already living here, with their unique cultures and spiritual lives. There were about 350 different cultures and more than 200 languages. Despite all of these differences, tribes that lived in the same region tended to have similar lifestyles.

The peoples of the Northeast lived in settled villages, raised corn and other crops, hunted, and gathered food, while northwestern peoples mainly relied more on catching salmon and other fish and gathering food to survive. The roaming tribes on the Great Plains and prairies hunted buffalo, while Pueblo tribes lived in close-knit, peaceful farming villages.

When white people arrived in North America, they did not understand native ways. The early settlers sent missionaries to convert the Native Americans to Christian religions. Catholic and Protestant churches set up missions. From colonial times, government policies aimed to stifle Native American religions.

By the late 1800s, Native American tribes across North America had begun to be conquered and were confined to reservations by the U.S. government. The government also sent thousands of Native American children to boarding schools, where they were told to live and act like white people. It was hoped that they would abandon their own cultures and religions and join white society.

Native Americans resented this idea. Walking Buffalo (Tatanga Mani), a Stoney of Alberta, said in the 1960s:

> You [whites] didn't understand our prayers. You didn't try to understand. When we sang our praises to the sun or moon or wind, you said we were worshipping idols. Without understanding, you condemned us as lost souls just because our form of worship was different from yours. . . . We saw the Great Spirit's work in everything: sun, moon, trees, wind, and mountains. Sometimes we approached him through these things. Was that so bad? I think we have a true belief in the supreme being. . . . Indians living close to nature and nature's ruler are not living in darkness.

Since the 1960s, there has been a renewed interest in native traditions, including art, music, language, and religion. Native Americans have taken charge of their schools and tribal governments. Recognizing at last the value of native religions, Congress passed the American Indian Religious Freedom Act of 1978. It pledges to "protect and preserve the inherent right of American Indian, Eskimo, Aleut, and Native Hawaiian people to believe, express, and exercise their traditional religions." This legal protection includes helping tribes gain access to their burial grounds, sacred objects, and land that is significant for ceremonies.

Ancient customs are an important part of Native American cultures today. These traditions, with their reverence for nature and a balanced life, have much to teach people of all backgrounds and beliefs. The chapters that follow show some important beliefs and customs of five major groups of Native Americans—those in the Northeast, South, Southwest, Great Plains, and West—a heritage that lives on today.

Chapter

2

Northeastern Tribes

Throughout North and South America, the religious traditions of Native American tribes were influenced by their geography, climate, food supply, and other factors. Whether they were hunters, farmers, gatherers, or wanderers, Native Americans needed a detailed knowledge of the land around them. Tribal legends attached meaning to particular places. The things that people needed to survive became the focus of prayers. For Native Americans of the Northeast, special importance was attached to planting time and harvesting crops, especially corn.

The northeastern tribes lived in the present-day states of Maine, New Hampshire, Vermont, Massachusetts, Rhode Island, Connecticut, New York, New Jersey, Pennsylvania, and in the Great Lakes region. Lush forests of pine, birch, oak, maple, ash, cedar, elm, nut, and fruit trees blanketed the land and mountains. The eastern lands were also dotted with many ponds, lakes, and rivers. A variety of wild plants, animals, and fish provided food. There are four distinct seasons that occur within this area, including a cold winter when crops could not be grown, and a colorful autumn.

Opposite:
The chief spiritual leader of the Algonquian-speaking Native Americans was the shaman. The shaman claimed to receive his mystical healing powers from dreams and visions. Here, a shaman shakes a ceremonial rattle while chanting a special incantation.

Many northeastern tribes spoke languages that stemmed from the Algonquian family of languages. Among the best-known Algonquian tribes were the Pequot, Narragansett, Nipmuk, Wampanoag, Mohegan, Penobscot, Passamaquoddy, Maliseet, and Abenaki. Another family was the Iroquoian, which included five nations by the 1500s: The Seneca, Oneida, Cayuga, Onondaga, and Mohawk. They lived mostly in what is now New York State and southern Canada.

The northeastern tribes tended to live in groups or clans made up of related families. They built homes and villages, but they moved about in the same area to set up hunting and fishing camps during different seasons. While men fished and hunted for game, the women gathered wild plants and did most of the planting in the villages. They raised corn, beans, squash, pumpkins, sunflowers, and tobacco.

Creation Stories

Northeastern tribes believed in a number of gods, called *manitos* or *manitous*, including a powerful creator who had made the world and showed his spirit through nature. The Iroquois creative force was called *Orenda*. Some of the Algonquian groups named their creator *Cautantowwit*, the great Southwest god who was believed to have made humankind and gave people the first seeds to grow plants. Among the Abenaki, this creator was *Odzihozo*, "the man who made himself"; to the Lenape, he was *Kishelemukong*, "who creates us by his thoughts." Other gods represented the souls of the dead; still others were associated with the sun, moon, stars, air, fire, and various animals.

The northeastern tribes had different creation stories, but many groups in these Eastern Woodlands shared the idea that the world was created on top of a giant sea turtle. In the Lenape story, the Creator lifted a turtle from the sea. Starting as an island, it grew to become the continent of

North America. The first man and woman sprouted from a tree on the turtle's shell as the Creator made the rest of the universe—sun, moon, stars, wind, plants, and animals.

The Iroquois creation story also involves a turtle. It says that before the Earth was created, people lived in the sky above an ocean with no land. Sky Chief and Sky Woman were expecting a baby, but one day Sky Woman fell through a hole in the sky and plummeted toward the ocean. Birds swooped beneath her, then laid her safely onto the back of a large turtle. While she was falling, Sky Woman grabbed roots and plants in the Sky World and planted these in soil on the turtle's back.

The Ojibwa (also called Chippewa) and Ottawa people who lived around the Great Lakes had a different creation story. In it, the Great Spirit dreamed of a world and made fire, wind, water, and the rocks, followed by the sun, moon, earth, and stars. Then the plants, flowers, birds, reptiles, fish, and non-human mammals were created—and finally, humans. Into all things, He breathed the spirit of life, and to humans, He gave the special power to dream. At first, this new world was peaceful and well balanced. A great flood came, and Sky Woman was sent to Earth to help the people. Landing on the turtle's back, she spread a mound of earth that became full of life. That place, known to the Ojibwa and Ottawa as the "place of the great turtle's back," is where present-day Lake Michigan and Lake Huron meet.

Creation stories were often retold at feasts held at certain times every year, including spring, late summer during the corn harvest, and midwinter. Ceremonies were also held at hunting and planting times and to mark important events in people's lives—receiving and changing names, puberty (adolescence), marriage, and death. Spiritual leaders and rulers—or chiefs—of allied tribes, called sachems, led these events. Many of the northeastern tribes worshipped in group settings called powwows, an Algonquian word that means "meeting." These special occasions included the retelling of tribal stories. Ceremonial pipes were used during these celebrations because it was believed that rising smoke carried people's messages up to the spirit world.

Spiritual Leaders

To become a spiritual leader, a person fasted (went without food) and had visions, often through dreams, during the years he or she spent learning about customs and rituals (religious ceremonies) of the tribe. Teenagers set out on spiritual journeys, called vision quests, in remote places where they prayed for a personal guardian spirit. Leaders often used this spirit—usually an animal—as part of their new, sacred name. Many tribal members thought the Creator showed his power through spiritually gifted people. Religious leaders, called shamans or medicine men, were called upon during times of ceremonies, illnesses, and difficulties for the tribe.

Among the Iroquois, The Peacemaker (Deganawidah) was both an outstanding religious leader and prophet during the 1400s. As a young man, he had dreamed of a cliff on which stood a gigantic fir tree with branches stretching into the sky. An eagle lingered near the top, while a snowy white material covered the ground below. The Peacemaker said the tree stood for the Native Americans and the cliff stood for peace, while the eagle was a guardian spirit. Traveling for miles on foot and by canoe, he shared his vision of love and friendship with the other Native Americans of the region. In Mohawk country, he met the noble chief Hiawatha. Together, they worked to unite the five tribes, who promised to live in peace and friendship among themselves.

When spiritual leaders took part in tribal ceremonies, they wore special animal skins, usually from the deer, moose,

An Iroquois chief, Etow Oh Koam, or King of the River Nation, portrayed by John Simon.

or bear that lived in the Northeast. They painted symbols on their skins and sacred objects, using colors that fit the occasion. Pigments for paint came from minerals, clay, charcoal, and plants. The Native Americans used red to represent life, yellow for the sun, white for the world, black for death, brown for earth, and green for growing plants. People who were in mourning often painted their faces black to show reverence for the dead. They would do this for as long as one year.

Ceremonial Traditions

Songs and dances were important in celebrations or rituals. Music was played on drums, flutes, and rattles, often made from empty gourds. As the sachem chanted or danced, others around him might sing prayers. They sometimes also threw hides, food, and ornaments into the fire as a sign of sacrifice. The Narragansett and other tribes had a special ceremony in which they gave up such things as beads, skins, cooking utensils, and hatchets. This was somewhat like the gift-giving potlatch ceremony held by Native Americans of the Northwest Coast. The more people gave, the more they were praised.

The Ojibwa tribe of the Great Lakes region had a Medicine Lodge Society, or Grand Medicine Society, that carried out the special medicine dances or rituals (*Midewiwin*) of early spring and late fall. These groups had secret healing rites for curing many different illnesses. Members of the Medicine Lodge Society were taught how to use the plants and herbs that were known to be traditional remedies for sickness. Among the Iroquois, painted masks called False Faces were worn by healers during special ceremonies. The False Face Societies played a major role in the healing process. False Face masks were carved only from a living tree, as the Iroquois believed that this way the mask retained part of the tree's spirit.

Thanksgiving ceremonies were also important throughout the year. The Ojibwa, who harvested wild rice, offered the first grains they found during harvest season to the Great Spirit. When hunting, men thanked their animal prey for giving up their lives so that they and their families could eat. Hunters treated the bones of dead animals with respect. It was considered wrong to take more food or other resources than one needed to live, as they believed the world must stay in careful balance.

The Green Corn Dance, or Green Corn Ceremony, which was also a southeastern tribal custom, was a major annual event for the Iroquois people. During that time, people prayed for a successful harvest as well as for their personal spiritual growth. They thought about how to improve themselves and how to learn to use their talents and skills to help the group.

False Face masks, which were carved entirely from a living tree, played a major role in the healing rituals of the Iroquois. This False Face mask was made by a Mohawk.

Life After Death

All the northeastern tribes believed there was a life of the spirit after death. The Lenape thought that after death, a person's soul traveled to paradise along a path of stars in the sky—the constellation we call the Milky Way. The stars on the path were looked upon as "footprints" that have been made by previous souls.

Ojibwa burial customs demonstrated their belief in an afterworld. Bodies of the dead were placed in their graves in a sitting position, facing west. In the grave were things one would need for a journey—a blanket, kettle, flint to start a fire, and moccasins for a man; for a woman, an axe, blanket, kettle, and moccasins. The Ojibwa said souls left the body right after death and began a journey west. Along the way, the dead found strawberries (heart berries) to eat before they had to cross a rapid stream with a wobbly bridge. The end of the journey was the land of the spirits. There were beautiful waters and abundant food, and Native American ancestors waited with welcoming songs and dances.

Threats to Ancient Ways

Because of their location, the northeastern tribes were among the first to have contact with white settlers during the 1500s. When Christian missionaries arrived in Iroquois country, a Seneca chief named Sa-go-ye-wat-ha (Red Jacket) said to them:

> Brother, we do not understand these things. We are told that your religion was given to your forefathers, and has been handed down from father to son. We also have a religion which was given by our forefathers, and has been handed down to us, their children. We worship in that way. It teaches us to be thankful for all favors we receive; to love each other and be united. We never quarrel about religion, because it is a matter which concerns each man and the Great Spirit. Brother, we do not wish to destroy your religion or take it from you; we only want to enjoy our own.

Nonetheless, Native Americans were not left alone to practice their traditional ways. Wars, diseases brought from Europe, and the seizing of their lands left tribes smaller, poorer, and less united. Territories were sharply reduced, and they were sent to live on tracts of land called reservations.

The Oneida group of Iroquois were among the many tribes that lost almost all of their homeland to European settlers. To the Oneida—whose name means "people of the standing stone"—a certain stone on their land marked the place where their ancestors found the right path to a fertile place to live. In 1784, the governor of New York agreed the Oneida were entitled to six million acres. Throughout the years, however, U.S. government policies reduced the tribe's holdings to just thirty-two acres. After a struggle, the Oneida managed to keep the land on which their sacred stone is located. A nearby longhouse—the traditional Iroquois dwelling—is still used for ceremonies and council meetings. Today, the Oneida are attempting to regain much of their homeland through legal means.

A belief in the sacredness of burial grounds remains part of Native American life. The Pequot of Connecticut, along with Native Americans all over North America, have gone to court to reclaim ancestral bones that were placed in museums. Moonface Bear of the Paugussett tribe of Connecticut said: "For so many years, the bones of our dead were treated like dinosaur bones—on display. They were dug up and put in a museum. Why our grounds? Not only has a living culture been taken away, but respect for the dead." Moonface Bear and others say it insults their religion to dig up burial sites. They want museums to return bones and other Native American objects. The Smithsonian Institution in Washington, D.C., and other museums have said they will try to find out where the objects in their possession belong. They have said they will return them to the tribes, in accordance with a newly enacted federal law called the Native American Graves Protection and Reparation Act of 1990.

As Native Americans reclaim their heritage, they continue their ancient ways. The Iroquois still watch over the "fire that never dies" out of respect for the sun in their council house on Onondaga land in the northeastern woodlands. The council still meets at this sacred place. And throughout the winter, when the frozen lakes of the Northeast glisten in the moonlight, Iroquois storytellers begin the old tales with the words, "Listen my children while the fire glows red, and the shadows come and go, and I will tell you the story of . . ."

Chapter

3

Southern Tribes

The southern tribes—including the Cherokee, Nanticoke, Creek, Choctaw, Seminole, Catawba, Timucua, Chitimacha, Tuscarora, Natchez, Apalachee, Santee, Chickasaw, and Shawnee—enjoyed lush, fertile homelands that stretched from present-day Maryland and Virginia to states east of the Mississippi River—Tennessee, Alabama, Mississippi, Louisiana, North and South Carolina, Georgia, and Florida.

Tribal names were given by one tribe to another, by white people, and by a tribe itself. For this reason, a tribe usually had several names. Many of the names the southern tribes chose for themselves meant "children of the sun." The long summers in the South were hot, and the land had rich natural resources of water and thick forests of oak, pine, cypress, fruit, and nut trees. Crops like corn, beans, squash, and tobacco grew well in the rich soil and sunshine. Plenty of animals, wild plants, and fish provided other sources of food. The beauty and abundance of the South led many tribes to call their lands "fruitful earth."

Thousands of years ago, the ancestors of the southern tribes, called Mississippians, kept an eternal flame burning

Opposite:
Many southern tribes, as well as tribes in other areas of North America, performed ritual dances to enhance the spiritual feelings of tribal members.

in their religious temples. This flame was a sign of respect for the sun, which showed its power on Earth through fire. Archaeologists have found ancient sites that had elaborate burial grounds and enormous mounds that contain objects testifying to a strong ceremonial life. The custom of keeping a fire year-round was continued by the peoples that followed. For example, the Cherokee kept a fire in their village house, putting it out and starting a new one only once a year, on New Year's Day. The people of the Mississippian culture, which lasted between about A.D. 800–1500, also believed in life after death. They thought a person was sent to another world to be either rewarded or punished.

Creation Stories

Creation stories differed from tribe to tribe and often featured the sun in a major role. Among the Cherokee (or as they call themselves, *Ani-yun'wiya*—"principal people"), it was said that long ago, people and animals understood each other and lived together in a sky of solid rock. As this sky became overcrowded, various animals left to explore new worlds and found a sea and the Earth below. Eventually, humans came from the Upper World to live in this new place, the Earth, which they called This World. Still other creatures lived in a third world, called the Lower World.

On Earth, the first man and woman, Kana'ti and Selu, had a son and raised another child, called Wild Boy, who was often mischievous. One day, the two boys picked up a rock and a number of animals escaped from their hiding places beneath it, which is why humans must now hunt for them. At some time, humans lost their ability to hear and speak the languages of birds and animals. They could understand only other humans.

In the Creek story, the world began as a dark, sunless place. Only one side of the Earth had sun, and the people there were too greedy to share it. When the fox tried to snatch a piece of the sun in his mouth, it burned its skin, leaving it black. Next, the opossum tried to carry a piece of sun on his bushy tail, but it burned, leaving the scanty tail opossums have today. The spider tried carrying it in a sack but could not lift it high enough. At last, the buzzard succeeded in placing the sun high in the sky, but now, he has a bald, red head. The Creek believe that the buzzard is an honored animal for this reason. They avoid killing buzzards, as well as wolves, rattlesnakes, or other animals they consider sacred.

Good and Evil Spirits

The southern tribes viewed the world as having both good and evil spirits. Good ones brought health, prosperity, and successful hunting, while bad ones brought on sickness, early death, and poor crops. Special objects, practices, and ceremonies were meant both to call up the good spirits and send bad ones away.

To avoid bad spirits, people also paid attention to tribal taboos—forbidden acts. These included sleeping in a position that faced west, where bad spirits lived. Instead, people slept facing east. People avoided looking at animals with traits they wanted to avoid, such as the mole with its poor

Masks, such as this Cherokee "booger" mask, played a central role in many Native American rituals. Masks were used to perform tribal stories, to summon or chase away spirits, and to adorn elaborate costumes for celebration.

eyesight. Screech owls were shunned because their shrill cry was a prediction of death. Food was cooked well, until no blood remained.

To attract good spirits, magic charms (amulets) were popular. Many Cherokee amulets were made of polished quartz and were used to bring luck. Each tribe cherished its medicine bundles—animal hides holding powerful spiritual objects and amulets used by the tribe. These bundles were guarded and used only by shamans—men or women with spiritual powers—on special occasions. When not in use, the bundles were hidden. These ceremonial bundles might also contain rattles, stone tubes used to administer herbs or plant medicines, and the sacred pipe (calumet). The ornaments worn during ceremonies, such as deer headdresses and bear claw necklaces, might also be stored in the bundles.

Sacred Rituals

Rituals took place often among the southern tribes. To please the sun, a bit of food was fed to the cooking fire at each meal. Before hunting, men often fasted, prayed, and purified themselves. They drank a brew of a strong tea plant called the black drink, which was prepared by important women in the tribe. This ritual was thought to help hunters find more turkey, deer, and other game.

After killing an animal, the hunter spoke to its spirit, saying words of comfort and explaining that human beings need food. Sometimes the hunter sprinkled some of the animal's blood on the ground to attract other animals.

The black drink used before hunting had other important purposes. Men who had passed through puberty drank it from gourds or conch shells at certain times of day, at council meetings, and during the Green Corn Ceremony. The Creek tribe believed that the Great Spirit had given them this drink.

For the Seminole, who lived in present-day Florida, fire and water were sacred. These elements were used often in Seminole ceremonies, as when they bathed in cold streams. This custom began shortly after birth, when infants were bathed in cold water. The Seminole also kept a fire burning constantly in their village. They extinguished it briefly during their summer harvest celebration, then started it once again for the coming year.

For the Seminole of present-day Florida, rituals marking nature's bounty were very important. This engraving shows the summer harvest being transported by river.

As with many tribes, those in the South placed a great amount of importance on dreams. They believed the body and spirit were separate and that the spirit could leave the body at night during sleep, to experience dreams. When the peace pipe was smoked, the smoke was thought to carry messages to spirits in the sky.

The Green Corn Ceremony

For these southern tribes, the Green Corn Ceremony, or Green Corn Dance, of late June to mid-July was the most important annual ritual. The Creek, Cherokee, and other tribes called it the *busk* (for *buskita* or *puskita*, meaning "fast"). Before the new corn appeared on the stalks, people fasted and readied themselves for the gift of corn that gave life to their people. For eight days, these tribes replaced old or broken pottery and other household items to make way for fresh ones. Homes were cleaned inside and out and fires were extinguished.

A cleansing of people's minds and hearts also took place at this time. The tribal clans met to talk about the past year and plan what they could do better in the future. It was a time to forgive each other for past complaints and restore peace and order to their world. Again, the black drink was used to give people strength and to cleanse their insides. The drink made people sick to their stomachs so that they vomited. Shamans directed the taking of this drink and led the public prayers and ceremonies during the festival.

A special speech was given in the village square by the *yatika*—the long talker. The *yatika* spent much time getting ready for this annual event. Everyone came to attention as he spoke the opening words: "Ta-a-a intukastci . . . "

For the Seminole, the Green Corn Dance signified the beginning of the new year. Many rituals were held during this event, which usually lasted four to six days. The leading holy man and his helpers took sweatbaths—religious steam baths that took place in a special sweathouse—before the Green Corn Dance. Participants danced around a fire. After a feast came a fast of several days, and the drinking of teas. The tribe honored the contents of the medicine bundles. People settled any arguments and repaid debts or favors. At the end, they broke their fast and ate some of the new corn crop for the first time.

A highlight of the Cherokee ceremony was a special three-hour daytime dance by women wearing splendid, ornamental costumes. The men danced in the evening, and on the third day, warriors and young men performed a long dance on the square. Singers accompanied the dancers' footwork. Tortoiseshell rattles were often played to accompany the singing.

Different tribes had their own ways of doing the Corn Dances. The Seminole rituals included more than forty dances. As with other Native American ceremonies, the words and movements were done to inspire people toward spiritual thoughts and feelings. Their main purpose was not entertainment.

Games such as stickball might be played during the festival. A peace ceremony ended the event, as people asked each other for forgiveness and stopped holding any grudges toward others. A new tribal year thus began with feelings of unity and goodwill. Songs of friendship, peace, and harmony were sung, and the peace pipe was smoked as a sign of this spiritual renewal.

Death and Burial

As there were joyful ceremonies, there were also mournful ones at times of death. The Choctaw placed their corpses outside to dry in the sun. They believed that only the bones should be buried, with no skin remaining. Special baskets or pottery containers held the bones of the dead, which were then put in special houses or funeral mounds. Solemn dances were performed for the dead. In common with other tribes throughout North America, dying people often said their last words in the form of a song. Annual ceremonies were held to honor the dead. During Choctaw ceremonies, people covered their heads, fasted, and made retreats— solitary visits away from the tribe for spiritual purposes.

Lost Homelands

The southeastern tribes lost many of their customary ways and their homelands in the early 1800s. During those years, the U.S. government opened their land to white settlers. Strong efforts were made to save the land by educated, well-spoken leaders such as the Cherokee John Ross. (Ross was president of the Cherokee nation and English was his first language.) Despite these efforts, however, these tribes continued to see their lands cut smaller and smaller. The U.S. government told them that they would be "removed"— stripped of their homelands and sent to live on an unfamiliar reservation in Oklahoma.

Heartsick and beaten, the tribes left, one after another. The Cherokee, however, managed to stay on their lands until 1838. Then, nearly 5,700 Cherokee died on a forced 800-mile trip west that spring. Their tragic journey, taken both by boat and on foot, was called the Trail of Tears because many Cherokee people fell dead to the frozen ground, marking it like teardrops.

Once in Oklahoma, the southeastern tribes had to reorganize and try to resume their traditions. Eventually, the "five civilized tribes" (as the Cherokee, Choctaw, Seminole, Chickasaw, and Creek were called because of their acceptance of many of the white man's ways) learned to live in their new surroundings. They started schools, newspapers,

The Cherokee tribe's 800-mile journey through harsh weather and rugged terrain is now known as the Trail of Tears, named for the tragic loss of life that it caused.

and a tribal government. They also held on to their spiritual traditions. While the Cherokee were no longer near their sacred sites, such as Red Clay Spring in Tennessee, they still had their oral history and values. To this day, new generations learn about the Cherokee belief that everyone should be of a good, or positive, mind. They try to turn anything bad that happens toward a better path. Such ideas give strength and hope to the descendants of these "children of the sun."

Southwestern Tribes

The American Southwest is a land of deserts, flat-topped hills called mesas, and striking sunsets. For thousands of years, it has been home to peaceful pueblo-dwelling Native Americans, including the Zuni and Hopi. The Apache and the Navajo who called themselves *Dine'*—"the people"— arrived in the Southwest in the 1400s. Today, these tribes still live in present-day Arizona, New Mexico, Utah, and Colorado. Spiritual traditions, especially among the Hopi, have been carefully preserved since ancient times. Many sites on their lands are considered sacred.

Before A.D. 400–500, the ancestors of the Pueblo peoples were called the Anasazi. Old caves where they once lived show that the Anasazi believed in life after death. People were buried with their clothing, baskets, pottery, ears of corn, and spears, among other things. Anasazi villages had oval or square pit houses, which were dug in the ground, and used for ceremonies.

Opposite:
Ancient Anasazi ruins glow in the light of New Mexico's Chaco Canyon. Believing in an afterlife, the Anasazi built elaborate chambers in which people were buried with many of their precious belongings.

After the 1200s, the Pueblo lived in settled villages on their hilltop mesas. They survived by farming corn through irrigation and gathering other kinds of food. The Pueblo explained that they arrived on Earth after traveling through a dark underworld, and then four other worlds. Finally, they emerged onto the sunlit Earth, where they had a Sun Father and Moon Mother. On Earth, they found the life-giving sun, but also many problems. Good spirits, as well as evil ones, existed on Earth.

Creation Stories

Creation stories explained the life cycles of the plants and creatures that lived in the Southwest. Some stories said that humans used four types of sacred trees to climb up from the underworld. A number of mountains and other places that were part of ancient tales were visited for religious purposes. For the Hopi, the point at which they came up from the underworld was the bottom of the Canyon of the Little Colorado River where it meets the Colorado River.

Among the Apache, Opler was the Great Spirit or Life Giver. White Painted Woman was a symbol for Mother Earth. Mountain Spirits of the Sacred Mountains were also important to the Apache, and masked dancers represented them in ceremonies.

In the Navajo creation story, mountains were created by First Man and First Woman. They journeyed through three different worlds before they reached the Earth, called Glittering World. By joining other Holy People—including Changing Woman—day, night, and the seasons were made. They also made the first hogan, the round traditional home of the Navajo. Changing Woman used her own skin and some corn to make the four Navajo clans. These clans lived amid four sacred mountains, now called San Francisco Peak, Mount Taylor, Bianca Peak, and La Plata Mountains.

Hopi men perform the sacred Snake Dance. This nine-day ritual was held in August to pray to the God of the Clouds for the rain that was so precious to inhabitants of the desert Southwest.

Appeals to the Spirits

Life in a dry, desert area made rain and water vital for the Southwest tribes. Without water, people could not survive. Many Southwest tribes often prayed for rain, celebrated its coming, and asked for the blessing of rain powers or cloud spirits. The Tewa-Hopi had a rain-power ceremony.

The Hopi held a nine-day Snake Dance in August to pray to the God of the Clouds for rain. The Snake Dance took place every other year, alternating with the Antelope Dance. Members of the Snake and Antelope societies took part in the ceremony. Priests led the dancers onto the village square, where they held the snakes, usually rattlers, and stroked them with special eagle-feather wands.

A Hopi chant about water, used all year, says:

Ho wondrous water,
Ho wondrous water,
Giving new life to the drinker . . .
Giving life to the people.

When getting ready for various ceremonies, the Pueblo went into their underground ceremonial chambers called kivas. They also used these rooms to store sacred objects and train men studying to be Hopi shamans. Some ceremonies were conducted in kivas.

Many people have seen Hopi kachina dolls. Kachina comes from a word that means "those from over the horizon." For the Pueblo people, these are supernatural beings—the spirits of those who have died. They have the power to bring crops and other good things. The dolls were used to teach children about religion. Adults also dressed as kachinas for certain ceremonies.

Rites and Ceremonies

A joyful ceremony of the Pueblo people was the annual Basket Dance. Beautifully woven baskets were used to show thanks for the life-giving harvest. Priestesses took part, chanting in a circle in the plaza, while young women carried baskets. They blessed the lives of women. At the end, the

young women threw baskets in the air, and young men scrambled for the prizes that toppled out on to the ground.

Thankfulness for their food was also part of the Navajo tradition. Cornmeal was sacred to them, as it was to the Pueblo. At a wedding, the bride's grandmother would give the newlyweds a basket of cornmeal. By exchanging a pinch of cornmeal during the ceremony, they hoped to gain the blessings of the spirit world. At Hopi weddings a "trail of life" (cornmeal) led from the groom's home to the bride's.

Hopi newborns were blessed on their naming day with a sacred ear of corn called Mother Corn. Navajo parents held their new baby's head toward the fire to thank the spirits. When a baby laughed for the first time, the person who caused the laughter brought food for a party. This tradition was thought to make a child unselfish.

Striving toward certain virtues was a constant goal for the Navajo. The Navajo Blessingway rite was one of the chantways, or special ceremonies, used to restore *hozho*—meaning harmony, happiness, goodness, and beauty. Often, such rites were used to get rid of evil or illness. The Navajo thought all people should work for *hozho*.

With harmony, balance, and order came beauty, according to Navajo thinking. Sickness was viewed as a sign that balance had been upset. To restore balance, the sick person took part in a ceremony lasting from two to fourteen days. These ceremonies took place in a hogan. Prayer wands, similar to those of the Pueblo, were used. Chants retold creation myths and the gods were asked to use their powers to heal.

A major part of the ceremony was the making of multicolor sand paintings (dry paintings) on the clean sand floor. The patient sat in the center of the floor while these were painted. Power was said to radiate from the center. The paintings symbolized divine spirits to whom the sick

Opposite:
This mural was painted on the wall of a Pueblo kiva around the year 1500. The walls of kivas were decorated to enhance these underground chambers, which were used for sacred ceremonies or to hold sacred objects.

person wished to become close. As the center of the painting reached the patient, the Navajo chanter would say,

> With beauty may I walk.
> With beauty before me, may I walk.
> With beauty behind me, may I walk.
> With beauty above me, may I walk.
> With beauty below me, may I walk.
> With beauty all around me, may I walk.
> In old age wandering on a trail of beauty, lively may I walk.
> In old age wandering on a trail of beauty, living again may I walk.
> It is finished in beauty.
> It is finished in beauty.

The Hopi, too, handed down their ideas about nature, peace, and harmony, saying that these were on the sacred stone tablets given them by the Great Spirit, Massau'u. Hopi beliefs are described in a letter that the Hopi leader Thomas Banyacya wrote to President Richard Nixon in 1970:

> The white man, through his insensitivity to the way of nature, has desecrated the face of Mother Earth. The white man's advanced technological capacity has occurred as a result of his lack of regard for the spiritual path and for the way of all living things. The white man's desire for material possessions and power has blinded him to the pain he has caused Mother Earth by his quest for what he calls natural resources. . . . The great Spirit said not to take from the Earth—not to destroy living things. The Great Spirit . . . said that man was to live in Harmony and maintain a good clean land for all children to come.

Enduring Ways

White people arrived in the Southwest during the 1500s. Despite intense efforts the Spanish and other missionaries made during those years to change their religion, Hopi traditions endured. The Hopi continued to practice their rites, even in secret. They have held on to their ways even to this day. Among these beliefs are ancient Hopi prophecies. Some of these prophecies said men would someday talk to each other by means of cobwebs through the sky, that they would travel in the air, and that two great wars would be fought by those bearing a swastika or rising sun. When the first bomb was dropped on Japan in 1945 at the end of World War II, Hopi prophets were reminded of another prophecy saying that a "gourd of ashes" would someday be dropped upon the Earth killing many people.

Navajo traditions also endure. Children still hear about the breath-of-life—how the first two people came to life when the wind blew breath into them. A Navajo holy man said in 1890: "It is the wind that gave them life. It is the wind that comes out of our mouths now that gives us life. When this ceases to blow, we die."

Like Native Americans elsewhere, southwestern groups have struggled to keep their lands. For the Taos Pueblo people, the Blue Lake in the mountains of northern New Mexico was sacred. For sixty-two years, they struggled to regain control of it. In 1970, the U.S. Congress voted to have 48,000 acres of the lake returned to the Taos. Standing beside President Richard Nixon as he signed the law, was religious leader Deer Bird (Juan de Jesus Romero), age ninety-seven, who had fought for this land all his life.

On their own lands, descendants of the ancient southwestern peoples can delight in the beauty of the region and their sacred sites. An Apache chant shows this joy:

> Big Blue Mountain Spirit,
> The home made of blue clouds,
> The cross made of blue mirage,
> There, you have begun to live.
> There, is the life of goodness,
> I am grateful for that made of goodness here.

Chapter

5

Plains Tribes

Through the years, the Plains Indians have had many well-spoken leaders who explained their views. Black Elk, an Oglala Sioux holy man, once said: "We regard all created beings as sacred and important, for everything has a *wochangi*, or influence. . . . We should understand well that all things are the works of the Great Spirit. We should know that He is within all things: The trees, the grasses, the rivers, the mountains, and all the four-legged animals, and the winged peoples; and even more important we should understand that He is also above all these things and peoples." These words show once again the Native American belief that God is in all of nature and the importance of harmony among all things.

Those living on the vast prairies and plains of North America witnessed many natural wonders. Their land stretched from the Mississippi River west to the Rocky Mountains. To the north was the Saskatchewan River of Canada, while the southern border was Texas. Vast mountains and rivers cut across this heartland of flat and grassy areas. Winters were often cold, but some regions had hot

Opposite:
Members of the
American Indian
Dance Theatre
perform the sacred
Eagle Dance of the
Plains Indians. The
eagle plays a central
role in many Native
American myths and
legends.

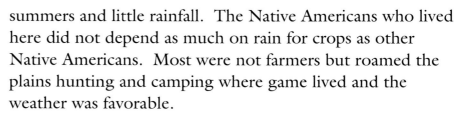
summers and little rainfall. The Native Americans who lived here did not depend as much on rain for crops as other Native Americans. Most were not farmers but roamed the plains hunting and camping where game lived and the weather was favorable.

The buffalo was the chief source of food, clothing, and shelter for the Plains tribes. These animals may have numbered up to 60 million at one time. They weighed about a ton (2,000 pounds) each and ate the short grasses that grew on the plains. Their meat provided food, while their skins were used for robes, blankets, and tipis. Plains Indians also hunted pronghorn (a kind of antelope), deer, elk, beaver, and birds.

Among the best-known prairie tribes were the Mandan, Osage, Pawnee, and Wichita. The Great Plains hunting groups included Arapaho, Blackfoot, Cheyenne, Comanche, Crow, Kiowa, and different bands of Sioux. One man who once lived among Plains Indians said of their beliefs: "Noble and beautiful ceremonies were created, having at their hearts truths universal to mankind; and nowhere in America were such mysteries loftier and more impressive than among the tribes of the Great Plains."

Slow Bull, an Oglala Sioux medicine man, stands with a ceremonial pipe on the Great Plains.

Creative Beings

The Plains tribes had originated in the East and kept some eastern customs while adding others suited to life on the plains. They respected spirits in animals and plants and in the wind, fire, earth, and rain. A creative force in nature, what white people began calling the Great Spirit, was part of their beliefs. The Blackfoot called their main spirit Nap (old man), while for the Sioux it was a group of spirits called Wakan Tanka, who had sent the buffalo for food.

Many creation stories of the plains speak of a vast flood that swept across the Earth. These stories often include a set of twins; one good, one evil, who changed life on Earth. The Sioux said that a great flood caused by a water monster took place in the early days of the Earth. An eagle saw a young woman climb a high hill to avoid drowning in the swirling water. He rescued her and carried her to his nest, where she was the only human survivor. She and the eagle had twins, a girl and a boy, and went to live on Earth after the water dried up. These were the ancestors of the Sioux.

In the Mandan story, people once lived underground near a large lake. A gigantic vine sprang from the underground lake to the Earth above. After some humans climbed up and saw the world above with its sun, animals, and plants, they persuaded others to join them. The Hidatsa, close relatives of the Mandan, had a similar story but told the separate origins of their three villages.

Vision Quests

Almost all Plains tribes encouraged individuals to go on a vision quest to find a guardian spirit helper. These quests were especially important to help men in hunting and war. At age fifteen, males gathered sacred objects into a medicine bundle to take on the quest. The bundle might hold corn, herbs, animal bones, stones, or sticks. The young men fasted beforehand and took a sweatbath to purify themselves. The wood-framed sweathouses, or sweatlodges, were topped with buffalo skins. Men chanted prayers after building a fire. They rubbed sage on themselves. Water was placed on hot rocks inside the building to make steam.

The Black Hills of South Dakota, Bear Butte (near present-day Rapid City), and Deer Medicine Rocks were important sites for a vision quest. It was said that the great Sioux leader Sitting Bull had his vision at Deer Medicine Rocks. Those who had an especially powerful spiritual experience on their quest sometimes shared it with the group through art, a dance, or music.

In 1911, Tatanka-ohitika (Brave Buffalo), a Sioux born in North Dakota, described his childhood experience:

> When I was ten years of age I looked at the land and the rivers, the sky above, and the animals around me and could not fail to realize that they were made by some great power. I was so anxious to understand this power that I questioned the trees and the bushes. It seemed as though the flowers were staring at me, and I wanted to ask them, "Who made you?" I looked at the moss-covered stones; some of them seemed to have the features of a man, but they could not answer me. Then I had a dream, and in my dream one of these small round stones appeared to me and told me that the maker of all was Wakan Tanka, and that in order to honor him I must honor his works in nature. The stone said that by my search I had shown myself worthy of supernatural help. It said that if I were curing a sick person I might ask its assistance, and that all the forces of nature would help me work a cure.

The Importance of the Circle

The circle shape was vital to the Sioux. This is one reason they dreaded the idea of living in square log houses, as white people wished them to after the 1800s. The square shape had no power in their belief system. For centuries, tipis had been round like bird's nests, and groups of tipis were set in circles—"the nation's hoop," as they called it. Black Elk wrote in his 1932 biography:

> Everything an Indian does is in a circle, and that is because the power of the World always works in circles, and everything tries to be round. In the old days when we were a strong and happy people, all our power came to us from the sacred hoop of the nation and so long as the hoop was unbroken the people flourished. The flowering tree was the living center of the hoop, and the circle of the four quarters nourished it. The east gave peace and light, the south gave warmth, the west gave rain, and the north with its cold and mighty wind gave strength and endurance. . . . Even the seasons form a great circle in their changing, and always come back to where they were. The life of a man is a circle from childhood to childhood and so it is in everything where power moves.

Ceremonial Traditions

A Crow Tobacco Society bundle. Tobacco played a key role in Crow ceremonies.

Many religious societies flourished on the plains. The men in the Crow Tobacco Society planted the tobacco and conducted the smoking ceremonies for the tribe. Among the Hidatsa and Mandan tribes, women participated in the

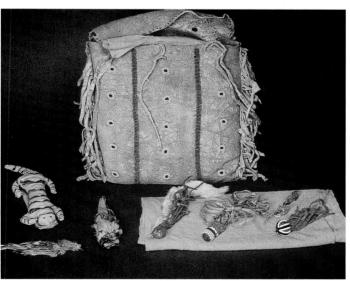

Female Buffalo Society. They performed special dances to attract the buffalo during the hunting season.

The Pawnee tribe's Hako Ceremony took place each spring. It was meant to promote friendship among different clans. A Pawnee holy man said, "With the Hako, we are praying for the gift of life, of strength, of plenty, of children being born to the tribe, and of peace."

Members of the Ponca, a Plains tribe found in Oklahoma, perform their Sun Dance. For many Plains tribes, this ritual took place annually and was regarded as one of the most important ceremonies of the year.

The yearly Sun Dance (also called the Medicine Dance) is a well-known spiritual custom. To the Sioux, it was *wiwanyag wachipi*—"looking at the sun," which was believed to be the source of life. The modern version dates back to about 1800, but the dance was built upon ancient rites. The Sun Dance had strong elements of warfare. Tribes held special prayers and dances to renew the Earth and its people, improve their ties with the sun and the animals, and bring visions to individuals. During this spring or summer ceremony, people gave thanks and prayed for special purposes.

A large pole or sacred cottonwood tree was set up at the center of the place chosen for the dance. This tree symbolized a connection between earth and sky. Male dancers often fasted before and during the ceremony. Some dancers used leather thongs to tie pieces of the skin on their chest to the pole. As they moved, the thongs cut their flesh, showing their courage. Among the Lakota Sioux, dancers moved so they always faced the sun. It was customary during the ceremony to give presents and various goods to friends and those in need.

The Cheyenne Sun Dance also aimed to keep strong herds of buffalo in their region. One of their sacred sites was the Black Hills of South Dakota. There, the Great Spirit Maiyun had received a sacred bundle of four arrows—two for war and two for hunting. Another annual Cheyenne ceremony was meant to renew these arrows.

An important Kiowa site in the Bighorn Mountains of Wyoming is their Medicine Wheel, dating back to about 1700. Boulders lay in a large circle with twenty-eight spokes coming out from the center. The Kiowa say it was made for Sun Dance ceremonies, celebrated with their friends, the Crow.

The Plains tribes also created the Ghost Dance. Started around 1888, the Ghost Dance reached its climax when Sitting Bull was killed on December 15, 1890, by police on a reservation in North Dakota. Sitting Bull was the leader of the Ghost Dance religion. The dance is still performed today among some tribes.

Like other groups, Plains Indians believed in life after death. The Assiniboine said each person had four souls:

Three died with the physical body while the last remained alive as a spirit bundle that would be released to Wakan Tanka after the friends of the dead person brought gifts. In his old age, the Sioux holy man, Black Elk, expressed no fear of death. He said that he would soon "pass from this world of darkness into the other real world of light."

Modern Plains Indians have maintained old spiritual practices, such as the Sun Dance, Ghost Dance, vision quest, and other ceremonies. Often, different tribes meet in summer powwows. Such customs give more meaning to life and help young tribe members learn and relive the old ways.

This elaborately designed coat was used by the Pawnee to perform the sacred Ghost Dance, a ritual that began in 1888 and is still performed today.

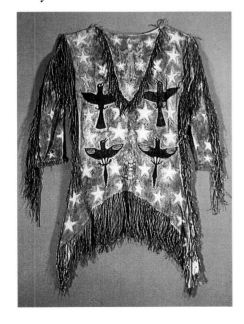

Chapter

6

Western Tribes

Various groups of Native Americans lived in the region stretching from the western plains to the Pacific Coast. Coastal Salish and northwestern Native Americans—Yakima, Colville, Kalispel, Kootenai, and Columbia tribes—lived in a rainy area of mountains and thick evergreens. They traveled by canoe, fishing and trapping salmon during the spring and summer. Autumn brought berries and nuts. Native Americans along the California Coast also enjoyed food from the sea. Plateau tribes—Nez Perce, Coeur d'Alene, Flathead, and Cayuse—fished, hunted, and gathered wild plants, while the Paiute and Shoshone in the Great Basin deserts often struggled to find food in a region that lacked good farmland and large game.

Spiritual customs reflected their different lifestyles. When a Paiute father heard the first cry of his newborn child, he ran as fast as he could far into the hills. This ritual was expected to give the child powerful legs for the endless up-and-down food hunts in this rugged territory. Because

Opposite:
Speaker's staffs, such as this highly detailed example, were carved from a single piece of wood and told important stories through the images they depicted.

women were important as food gatherers in the Plateau and Great Basin, they also had a larger role in tribal leadership, including religious rites.

Ceremonial Traditions

The Nez Perce and other tribes held thanksgiving ceremonies when the first salmon ran down the streams. Among the Suquamish-Duwamish groups near present-day Seattle, Washington, a special ceremony marked the day the first butter clams were harvested offshore. The Paiute celebrated the pine nut harvest with prayers and celebrations. These nuts, gathered from trees in their region, were needed for survival. They were roasted, then ground into flour for the harsh winters when food was scarce. Food was so welcome in the Great Basin that any good find led groups of families to gather for a thanksgiving ritual called a Round Dance.

The Nez Perce held their thanksgiving—*Q'eunyit*—for gathering nuts, berries, bitterroots, wild carrots, and camas bulbs. During these times, they prayed to *Hanyawat*, their Creator. The Earth was viewed as their mother, while every living animal, plant, or bird was a brother or sister.

The Kwakiutl of British Columbia had rituals and prayers for every important act of daily life. These rituals often involved the number four. During their Salmon Ceremony and other prayers to animals and plants, this tribe always used the phrase, "Friend, Supernatural One."

To cleanse themselves and pray, men used sweathouses, another custom they shared with Plains Indians. The lodges held aspects of the four elements—earth, fire, water, and air. The dome-shaped rooms were covered with bent willow saplings (the symbol of the Earth). When water hit the red-hot rocks, steam made the room hot and damp. Forming a circle, people in the lodge smoked the sacred pipe, singing songs and praying.

Respect for Nature

Despite the shortage of food in the Plateau region, people still took care not to upset nature. It was customary to replace something taken from the ground with something else. Native Americans who pulled roots or bulbs from the ground for food in this region might put back a shiny pebble. The Wintu of California believed one must respect all living things, including trees. When the Wintu needed fuel, they did not kill a tree. A Wintu woman said: "When we Indians kill meat, we eat it all up. When we dig roots we make little holes. When we build houses, we make little holes. . . . We shake down acorns and pinenuts. We don't chop down the trees. We use only dead wood."

A famous Nez Perce religious leader named Smoholla expressed his tribe's views during the 1850s. When white people told him the Nez Perce should take up farming, he said: "You ask me to plow the ground. Shall I take a knife and tear my mother's breast? Then when I die she will not take me to her bosom to rest. You ask me to dig for stone. Shall I dig under her skin for her bones? Then when I die I cannot enter her body to be born again. You ask me to cut grass and make hay and sell it and be rich like white men. But how dare I cut off my mother's hair?"

Guardian Spirits

As in other places, western Native Americans sought a guardian spirit. The Nez Perce called theirs *weyekin* and hoped that a special protector would come to them for a lifetime. As they reached their teen years, boys and girls set out alone to sacred areas in the mountains to pray and fast. They carried objects with spiritual significance, such as a sacred feather, on their quest. A vision might come in the form of an eagle, deer, bird, bear, or other animal while they prayed and fasted, according to custom. Those who developed special powers could become healers, religious leaders, or chiefs. Sacred sites for vision quests included the Kootenai Falls of Idaho (Salish-Kootenai), the Wallowa Lake in northeastern Oregon (Nez Perce), and Mount Adams in Washington (Yakima, Klikitat, and Sahaptian).

Joyful Gatherings

At winter dances in the Plateau, leaders thanked their spirit helpers and renewed their world. As in other Native American cultures, ceremonies were intended to develop pleasing relationships with the spiritual forces of the earth, sea, and

This necklace, made by the Kootenai of North America's Northwest region, was adorned with buffalo teeth.

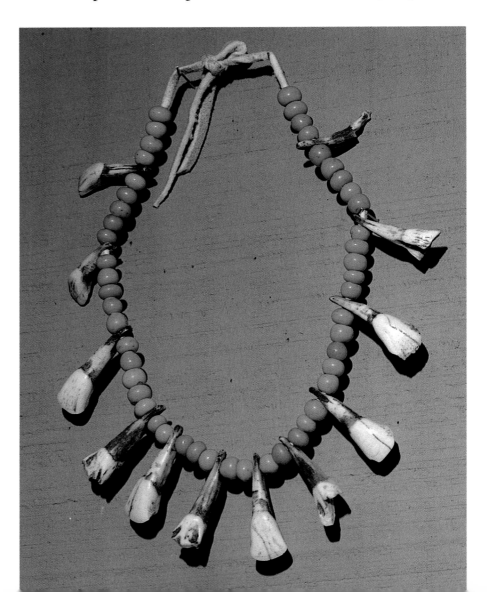

This elaborate Shoshone pipe is representative of those used by many Northwest Native Americans. Pipes were often smoked and shared during important ceremonies as a symbol of peace and unity among people.

animal world. Storytelling was part of these gatherings. In some tribes, people told stories of a mythical raven that had transformed the world before humans arrived. Other tales described how humans had gone from being good to a state in which they were greedy, upsetting the balance of the world and all of its creatures. Some coastal stories told of sea monsters from whom humans needed protection.

A popular coastal tradition was the potlatch. At this feast, guests listened to a family's history and stories about their clans and traditions. Songs and dances, using masks and other objects, portrayed this history. Guests received food and gifts from the host family. Elderly tribal members gave away their personal belongings at a potlatch before they died.

As in the Great Plains and some other regions, these Native Americans had sacred pipes, called calumets. The pipes were brought out during important occasions as a symbol of unity and peace. As someone placed grains of tobacco in the stone or clay bowl of the pipe, someone else told an important part of the tribe's creation story. Another man lit the pipe, making a prayer to the Earth and sky, as smoke rose above. The fire itself symbolized what Native Americans viewed as the Great Mysterious. Sometimes when smoking, the group spoke the words: "We are all related." This is the central idea that unites all believers.

Glossary

archaeologist Scientist who studies ancient civilizations—
the histories and cultures of the past.

blessingway rite Traditional Navajo ceremony meant to
promote harmony and goodness.

busk Name given by the Creek of the Southeast to the
annual Green Corn Ceremony (from *buskita* or *puskita*
for "fast").

calumet Sacred object, usually a decorated pipe made of
wood and clay-stone, used for peace ceremonies and
meetings with important purposes.

clan Social group of Native Americans that included several
households with a common ancestor.

creation stories Legends that describe how Earth and all
living things came to be.

culture The beliefs, values, and ways of life of a people.

Green Corn Ceremony Annual festival of the southeastern
tribes, including Cherokee and Seminole, held when the
first corn was ripe.

hozho A word that sums up the life goals of the Navajo—
harmony, joy, goodness, and beauty.

kachina A spirit being that, among the Hopi, stands for
the supernatural forces of life.

kiva Underground ceremonial chambers used by the
Pueblo peoples to prepare for ceremonies, store sacred
objects, and train shamans.

medicine bundle Animal skin containing sacred tribal
items, such as calumets, feathers, and medicine tubes.

myth Story passed on from generation to generation that
tells of supernatural events and gods, connected to a
group's religion or history.

powwow A conference or gathering of Native Americans; often characterized by feasts, dancing, and celebration.

reservation A tract of land that was set aside by the United States for a group of Native Americans. Usually, reservations were small plots of poor-quality land that were offered to Native Americans only after white settlers had seized their lands.

ritual Particular form of a ceremony that incorporated a series of acts; most often religious.

sachem Native American healer thought to be in contact with spirit world. Also refers to a ruler or chief of allied tribes.

sacred site Geographic place that has special religious meaning to Native Americans. It might be a mountain, lake, river, rock, or other site.

sand painting (dry painting) A picture of sacred figures made on the ground using crushed charcoal and sandstone powders. Used during healing ceremonies of the Navajo. Although it reached its highest development among the Navajo, sand painting was also practiced by the Hopi.

shaman Spiritual leader often called upon for healing.

Snake Dance Most important Hopi ceremony in which people pray for rain.

Sun Dance Annual summer ritual of the Plains tribes and other Native American groups to give thanks and renew tribal life.

sweathouse Small building in which religious steam baths are taken; also called sweatlodge.

taboo An action that is forbidden.

vision quest Journey first taken alone during adolescence to seek the vision of a spirit helper for one's lifetime.

Further Reading

Andrews, Elaine K. *Indians of the Plains.* New York: Facts On File, 1992.

Caduto, Michael, and Bruchac, Joseph. *Keepers of the Earth: Native American Stories and Environmental Activities for Children.* New York: Dodd, Mead, 1984.

Claro, Nicole. *The Cherokee Indians.* New York: Chelsea House, 1992.

Doherty, Craig A., and Katherine Doherty. *The Crow.* Vero Beach, FL: Rourke, 1994.

_____. *The Huron.* Vero Beach, FL: Rourke, 1994.

_____. *The Ute.* Vero Beach, FL: Rourke, 1994.

Grant, Bruce. *Concise Encyclopedia of the American Indian.* Avenel, NJ: Outlet Books, 1989.

Hirschfelder, Arlene, *Happily May I Walk: American Indians and Alaska Natives Today.* New York: Scribners, 1986.

Lee, Martin. *The Seminoles.* New York: Franklin Watts, 1989.

Sherrow, Victoria. *The Hopis.* Brookfield, CT: Millbrook Press, 1993.

_____. *Indians of the Plateau and Great Basin.* New York: Facts On File, 1991.

_____. *The Nez Percé.* Brookfield, CT: Millbrook Press, 1994.

Stan, Susan. *The Ojibwe.* Vero Beach, FL: Rourke, 1989.

Wood, Leigh. *The Navajo Indians.* New York: Chelsea House, 1991.

Index

✷

63

Photo Credits
Cover: ©Lynton Gardiner/American Museum of Natural History; pp. 6, 44: ©Theo Westenberger/Gamma Liaison; pp. 8, 13, 16, 31, 39, 46, 50, 52: Library of Congress; p. 10: ©Craig J. Brown/Liaison International; pp. 21, 23, 29, 49, 51, 57: ©Blackbirch Press, Inc.; pp. 26, 40: North Wind Picture Archives; p. 35: Courtesy Chickasaw Nation; p. 36: ©Gene Peach Photography/Liaison International; p. 56: ©Tom McHugh/Photo Researchers, Inc.